Curse of the Wampus, and other Short Spooky Stories of Piedmont North Carolina.

O.C. Stonestreet IV

Contents

Acknowledgments

I wish to take time to thanks several individuals and various groups that made this work possible. Mick and Terry Shinn who ignited the fire with the Shinnville Witch case years ago. I would like to thank St. James Episcopal Church, and especially Arlene Hayes for her years of service to the Shinnville Community. A special thank you goes to Carol Spetter for her years of friendship and research assistance with the St. James investigation.

A special thank you goes out to Ms. Beckee Garris of the Catawba Indian Nation for allowing me to visit and hear of the *Yehasuri* legend first-hand. I wish to thank the O'Neil family for their years of fun friendship along with all of the other members of the Mary Slocumb Chapter of the Daughters of the American Revolution. These patriot friends have kept the spirit of the American Revolution alive, and my spirit for historic investigation as well! Thank you to my family as a whole. They have put up with me all of these years while I have tackled many projects. Also, many thanks goes to Mrs. Deb Hicks of the MHS English Department for her kind help.

Finally, I want to acknowledge the continued support of the Mooresville Graded School System, the members of the Mooresville Museum, the Mooresville Public Library, and all of my friends and colleagues who strive to make our hometown great.

Dedication

This work is dedicated to all of my students… past, present, and future. For in your hands is the story of our history.

Mr. Stonestreet

Introduction

For years I have dabbled with folklore and local legends while at the same time researching and teaching factual history. Occasionally, I would take time out to do a bit of research on a topic if it interested me and do a seasonal article for the local paper around Halloween. I have even been pulled into a mystery a time or two while actually doing a historical investigation. The following is a collection of published articles and other stories that I have come across over the years. This small book is for the young and old to enjoy. It is my ernest wish to keep the stories and our local oral traditions alive for future generations to ponder.

O.C. "Chris" Stonestreet IV
March 29th, 2015

Curse of the Wampus

October 22nd, 1931 9:38 pm

Shiloh Township, North Carolina

Old Jim Mayberry was readying himself for bed after a solid day's work on the Stewart Farm. The bed seemed softer than usual he thought, or maybe it just seemed to be that way after binding a hundred bales of straw during the fall harvest. His large, callused hands showed the signs of wear and strength, much like his father's who had been a tenant farmer on the same piece of land years before. After washing his rough and weathered face in the basin, he put on his tattered cotton night-shirt and slid softly under the covers.

He thought as he yawned… "Ah, that's good" as he stretched with all arms and legs, hearing an occasional crack in his back.

Suddenly in the distance, Jim heard the sound of hounds coming fast from the direction of the Stewart's Store, which lay just across their large cotton field. "What's all this ruckus…?" Jim grabbed the tin lantern beside his bed, and opened the lamp's aperture as far is it would go as he leaned out of the window overlooking the field. By now the sounds were louder, dogs hollering, barking, and yelping the likes of which Jim had never heard before during his 40 years on the farm. He could see a whirl of dust as the commotion began to settle and become more intense in the center of the field, as if whatever the hounds were chasing decided that it didn't want to be chased anymore.

Jim heard a hound scream in pain as if being bitten by some unseen steel trap. Jim shown the light towards the sounds but could only see dirt, plants, and fur leaping into the air. Then he saw a hound being flung as if it was a rag doll being thrown by some ill-tempered child. A cry cut the crisp night air, a cry that made Jim's back shiver and his heart skip. He thought it sounded like a cross between a woman moaning in great pain, and that of a bear holler. Whatever it was, it started fighting back!

Jim's eyes were struck by a second beam, another lamp coming from the direction of the Stewart Store, and figured that it was Mr. Praite who had been renting the store's loft. Evidently, he too had been awakened by the grotesque sounds. Slipping on his dusty shoes, Jim headed out of the shack with a shotgun in one hand and the lantern in the other. He moved toward the sounds that now seem to be lessening with every step. Soon he found himself in a clearing in the middle of the field, no hounds or "other" to be seen. Jim heard Mr. Praite getting close and loudly yelled… "Hey… It's me Jim, Mr. Praite!"

Mr. Praite's beam came piercing over the ridge as he also entered the clearing made by the scuffle.

Out of breath, Mr. Praite heavily panted…

"Jim… wha, what's going on?"

"I don't know sir, something was 'mixin' with them hounds."

The two men looked around and saw cotton plants ripped and torn, with blood scattered over much of them.

"Jim, come here and look at this..." The yellowish beams of the two lanterns focused on the tracks. Hound tracks were all over the recently trampled ground. Then the two beams converged on some tracks that were not made by any hound. These strange tracks were almost a foot in length, and as wide as a man's hand. As the two men bent down, the light caught the glimmer of fresh blood in the divots where the claws had sunk deep into the reddish clay. Jim said in a low tone...

"Oh Lord, looks like that Wampus is back in these parts again Mr. Praite."

It is a strange tale that for over a century has haunted the Piedmont of North Carolina. Is the Wampus, or sometimes referred to as the "Santer," a real creature or "Cryptid" yet to be classified? Most say that it is either a wildcat or mountain lion if it exists at all. Others say it was just the imaginary creature conjured up in the mind of a newspaper editor who saw in a spoof the chance to make unclean money during a lull in newspaper sales; playing on the superstitions that pervaded the African-American community at that time. Yet, as this researcher has found out, the tale is more complex and extends well beyond the Appalachian Mountains.

In the Piedmont of North Carolina since the 1890s, there have been sightings of a large cat-like creature whose appearance has been known to shape-shift to other terrifying forms. Reports of a creature that could kill live stock along with full-grown hounds which were guarding them. Farmers, townspeople, and even priests noted a blood chilling howl "not of this earth" in the evenings when the autumn sun's shadow stretches long over the ground. In 1911 it was reported that the Wampus was "dreaded more than the satan" by the children around Clarkston, Georgia due to a rash of attacks that year.

The legend of the Wampus may go back even further into the oral traditions of Native Americans. Centuries ago the Algonquin Tribe tell of a *Otshee Monetoo,* (Manitou) or "evil spirit" that roamed the ancient forests. Several South American tribes claim a jaguar like creature '*Chak-Mool*' lurks in the jungle canopy at dusk to attack those who are traveling along the pathways between villages. The quest for the truth of this mystical creature goes on today. In the past few years, strange sightings around Lake Norman and the region has some people wondering if the Wampus has made a return to haunt the area once again.

Funky Factoid: The *Wampus* has also been called the *Santer* by early western settlers. Supposedly, the range of these cat-like creatures stretch into Tennessee and as far south as upper Florida. * There have even been reports of mountain lion (or puma) attacks as recent as 2014 in Florida. (Retrieved 07/09/2015) http://www.newsmax.com/TheWire/mountain-lion-attack-golf-course/2014/04/10/id/564779/

The Legendary Witch of Shinnville: Fact from Fiction?

A legend still persists in Shinnville, North Carolina which still haunts the locals. The legend of a grave not on Holy Ground, forever damned. A grave of a witch, whose soul still lurks in the shadows off of the old Mills Family Cemetery near St. James Episcopal Church. The Mills were one of the founding families of Shinnville almost two centuries ago. Owning large tracks of land, and operating several businesses, the Mills family were well-stablished and well-respected. The current St. James Church can trace its origins to the Mills' home where the first services were held. Later, an actual church was built on the edge of the Mills' property. A short distance from the church is the family cemetery. As the decades passed, the cemetery was finally added to the church property.

Arlene Hayes, a church member, recounts the haunting story she heard when she was just a little girl: " Outside of the cemetery wall, a small stone without a name exists... Mom said it was a witch who was killed and buried outside the wall." Naturally, this was an amazing story to hear when I interviewed Mrs. Hayes in 2012. Yet as time went on, a more interesting story unfolded.

There was, and still is, a headstone suspiciously outside the wall of the 200 year old cemetery. But with further investigation, and a bit of "digging" in the records, it seems likely that this was one of the rare surviving headstones marking the grave of a servant who had worked with the Mills family during the Antebellum Era. Not long after the interview, I was honored to be part of a team from the church to investigate the possibilities of lost or unmarked graves. Within weeks we were able to say, with some certainty, there were many graves outside of the original walls. So where did the story of the witch come from in such a quiet hamlet on the outskirts of Mooresville, North Carolina?

Several possible answers are plausible. During the Victorian Era, ghosts and spirits were all the rage. Spiritualism was extremely popular in Europe and America at the end of the 19th Century. For a price, "Mediums" or people claiming spiritual gifts, could contact dead loved ones, and some of the first "ghosts caught on film" pictures were made. Many of these mediums were later to be proven to be charlatans cruelly preying on the sorrow of others, and the photographs turned out to be double exposed film. The famed magician Harry Houdini spent years trying to shine the light on the business of spiritual deception. Possibly, the legend of the witch started during the 19th Century's spiritualist movement.

Another possible answer might be the person buried under the stone was a community outcast. It was common practice to deny those who committed murder, or suicide, burial in sanctified ground at that time. During the interview, Arlene mentioned that several key church history books have been lost. The answer may have been in one of the lost records. Or could the answer be as simple as a scary tale that church-going parents told their children to keep them out of the cemetery? One may never know.

Many established churches are now trying to save their history; both oral and documented. Churches like St. James are a true gem for genealogical research. Prominent family names found around the Mooresville area like Westmoreland, Mills, Shinn and Overcash can be seen gracing the stones in the cemetery yard. Poetic epitaphs and symbolism can still be seen from a century ago. St. James itself is a rare example of Antebellum architecture. Yet, with our ever mobile society, and the continued development of the region, some of the churches and their cemeteries risk being destroyed. Unfortunately some are simply abandoned and forgotten as time passes.

As far as the Witch of Shinnville and the childhood story that Arlene heard from her mother, it may have been a case of parents trying to keep their children in at night or away from the cemetery. A local "Bogeyman Story" of sorts? The truth is that no one knows for sure who is buried under the stone, but in a way their immortality is assured as long as the stories and the history is passed down to a new generation in Shinnville.

Funky Factoid: The term *"Hoodoo"* is a southern term. It is combined from African magical beliefs of Voodoo (or *Vodun)* brought over during the slave trade era, and country "folk magic."

A True Story Worthy of Mary Shelley's *Frankenstein*

A short distance down Corban Avenue in old Concord, North Carolina is the Old Lutheran Cemetery. One could pass by it and never notice it perched high among the wooded lots. Yet, a century and a half ago it was the setting for one of the strangest and most macabre occurrences in the region.

In the warm spring of 1856, a stranger wandered into the township of Concord. He claimed to be many things ranging from a simple clock repairman to a traveling Baptist preacher. However, just a few weeks after settling in the area, he claimed that he had knowledge as a healer and started calling himself Dr. Nugent. This, by itself, is nothing new for the early 19th

Century; an age of "snake oil" salesmen and petty practitioners of the medical arts. What made Dr. Nugent different was his methods of treating ailments like rheumatism and arthritic pains.

Not long after he started peddling homemade lozenges, some in the slave community started talking about strange people visiting the colored cemetery in the early night. Frightened, they passed along the information, yet nothing was taken seriously. "Old spooks and superstitions" were being put to rest in this new age of science and reason. This all would change in a ghastly way when it was reported that a man and several accomplices were seen exhuming the bodies of two young children in the Lutheran church's cemetery in May of 1857.

The infant children of North Carolina General W. C. Means had tragically died of a high fever and measles within several days of each other just the month before. A civic group went to investigate if there was any truth to the story. Sadly, they found the new graves had been disturbed. After opening the fresh graves, they found them empty of not only the bodies, but the small pine coffins as well. Outraged, this 'vigilance committee' pursued the trail to Dr. Nugent who was found deathly sick and in bed himself with fever, chest congestion, and measles. He made a full confession and went on to say that he, along with a man named Mr. Baugus, had exhumed some seventeen other bodies for the purpose of extracting certain body parts which held "medical remedies." After a short bedside trial, Dr. Nugent was found guilty; however, he would not live to see man's justice. He died while in the sheriff's custody. His body would be unceremoniously buried in an unmarked grave in a field on the outskirts of town a few days later. Mr. Baugus was tracked all the way to South Carolina, and then back to North Carolina where he was finally apprehended in Charlotte. Only the remnants from Maggie and Eugenia Means were ever found; small bits of teeth and bone in the pile of ashes.

Not long after these terrible local events, a national tragedy would see the deaths of many thousands of Americans in the Civil War of the 1860s. The Old Lutheran Cemetery lay in a state of disrepair for years as the church moved several blocks away during the Reconstruction Era. The story of the Means family tragedy was forgotten until recently. Now, members of the church are trying to save and reclaim this historic cemetery which holds not one, but two North Carolina Generals; and many others who served North Carolina with distinction in its early years.

Poignantly, the intricately carved stone marker of Maggie and Eugenia Means still stands as a reminder of the tragedy long ago. The names of the girls are almost unreadable due to the effects of time and the green lichen which now grows over the stone's surface.

Funky Factoid: Frankenstein's monster was technically a "flesh golem." The golem is a creature made of clay, stone, or any base material. Yet, through magical incantations it becomes animated. This legend has its roots in Judaic Folklore.

The Girl at the Underpass:
An Enduring Ghost Legend of Piedmont North Carolina

Many people growing up in North Carolina have heard of at least one indigenous ghost story. Out of the many ghosts stories that exist in our state, one stands out as probably having the most notoriety, that being "The girl at the underpass." I can remember back in 4th grade my teacher reading to us several North Carolina ghost stories on Halloween. "The Devil's Tramping Ground," the "Brown Mountain Lights," and "The Maco Light" to name a few. Yet, the one that made an impression on my young mind is the story of the young girl still trying to get home on a dark, rainy night.

There are many variations of the story, and as my research has turned up, similar stories can be found all around our country and even the world. The "Phantom Hitchhiker" and the "Ghostly Traveler" are stories that go back as far as the 17th century. As far as our local story, though there are variations, the general story goes like this…

One rainy evening in the spring a young man was driving to High Point. He had been on the road most of the day, traveling home from college. His eyes were sore, and his muscles ached from the long drive. "I'll be home soon," he thought. "Not too soon to see my old bed and mom's home-cooking!" He arched his back and stretched as the car raced along the pavement.

Soon, the driver approached the Highway 70 underpass right before the small township of Jamestown. In the distance he could see the figure of a young lady standing by the road. She was evidently in distress as she frantically waved to him for help. His car slowed down under the bridge, as he rolled down his window. "Need some help miss?" The girl approached the car and said "Yes, I'm trying to get home to High Point. Could you give me a ride?"

"Sure, headed that way myself... get in." The young lady glided around the car and quietly slid into the passenger seat. Looking straight ahead with a blank stare she said, "I'm late getting home from the dance, and Mom is going to be worried." "Car trouble?" the man asked, yet she did not respond. Being a southern gentleman, he did not ask further. He thought, "Maybe she got dumped by her date?"

As they drove on, he noticed her outfit seemed a bit old-fashioned in appearance as it dripped rainwater onto his leather seat. It wasn't long before they approached High Point. "Turn here," she suddenly said as they entered one of the older parts of town. "My house is down this road on the corner." The man pulled slowly up the gravel driveway. As the car came to a stop, he noticed the house was totally dark. "Odd" he thought as he got out of the car to politely open her door. When he reached her side and opened it, there was nothing there! "Maybe she got out and ran to the house, but how did she get by me?" He then went to the door and knocked, minutes passed, when a light was turned on and an elderly woman opened to the door. "Ma'am, I brought your daughter home. Is she okay?" The woman looked sad and said, "My dear boy, my daughter Lydia will never come home. She died in a car wreck coming back from a dance in 1923."

Ever since I heard this ghostly tale years ago, I have wondered if it was all just a story to scare kids on Halloween, or if there was any truth to the tale? One thing that stood out about this story is that, unlike many tales, this one had a specific location and date associated with it. Thus, some daring friends and I decided to venture one Saturday morning to see if Lydia's overpass was real. Sure enough, it is. However, the road has been rerouted, and the original "Highway 70 Underpass" is around a 100 feet away. The new bridge, as well as the original overpass, is covered with graffiti. Local teenagers consider it a place to hangout, and after viewing the markings, one realizes that they too know the legend. Lydia's name adorns the walls, painted in blood-red letters. It is an erie and secluded place as nature itself is reclaiming the old roadbed and tunnel of the overpass; weeds, briars, and kudzu are all about the area.

Being a thorough researcher, and wanting to sort "Fact from Fiction," I stopped by the local library where the librarians, Sue and Jamie, were helpful in confirming not only the legend, but also locating information that confirmed one 'Lidia' Jane "M..." did exist. According to Alice E. Sinks's, *Hidden History of the Piedmont Triad*, an official death certificate was issued stating that she was: "Born 1904 in High Point and died December 31, 1923, from fatal injuries from a motoring accident...." Certainly the tragic death of a vibrant nineteen year old girl from what must have been a T-Model accident, in a time when motoring accidents were few and far between, would have had a lasting impact on the close-nit community. It is easy then to see how such a legend could begin.

Many publications of North Carolina ghost stories mention specific and spectral accounts of people seeing the apparition over the past 80 years. The legend continues to this day in the small township of Jamestown, North Carolina. More recent sightings have Lydia appearing near the new overpass on dark and stormy nights; having moved over a bit to catch a ride.

Yet, as this researcher has found out, there is always a some kernel of truth to any legend. In final analysis, is Lydia a real apparition? I guess it depends on a person's belief in the paranormal. Maybe it is true that the ghostly Lydia is still desperately trying to get home to High Point after all.

Funky Factoid: Chances are Lydia was killed in a Ford 'Model T.' There were over 15 million Model Ts produced between 1913 to 1927. Top speed for many of the early models was only 40 mph… and that was going down hill.

A Monster in "Loch" Norman?

One of the most known "monsters" in the world is the Loch Ness Monster of Scotland. This serpent-like creature had been spotted for centuries by tribal peoples on the shores of the River Ness, well before the 7th Century A.D. when St. Columba recorded an account of the beast while converting the locals to Christianity. Likewise in the America's, there is the *"Ogopogo"* lake monster supposedly living in the Okanagan Lake of British Columbia, Canada. Ever since the 19th Century, locals and visitors have told of a dinosaur like creature whose long hairy neck shoots out of the cold water followed by fast moving and undulating ripples as the creature speeds along the surface of the lake. Many people believe these creatures are some form of lost *plesiosaur* (a large air breathing sea creature of the Jurassic Era) that survived the extinction of the dinosaurs millions of years ago.

Interestingly enough, Lake Norman in North Carolina has rather recently laid claim to "Normie," the lake monster. Sightings of this beast have been reported over the last thirty years by various locals and tourists alike. One wonders how a lake that has only been in existence since 1963 could lay claim to such a monster? After all, Loch Ness and Okanagan Lake are extremely deep and millennia old. Lake Norman, which was created along the Catawba River, is nowhere near the vast depths that other known lakes which claim a resident monster. Yet cryptozooligists (or people that search for animals whose existence is yet to be proven by science) claim these animal may not live all year long in the lakes. Rather, these creatures live much of their lives in the seas. They occasionally work their way up the rivers during certain times of the year, possibly to spawn. After a short time closer to human kind, they instinctively find their way back to the deep blue waters of the oceans.

Could there be a large serpent-like creature in Lake Norman? One can never be sure. The lake has laid claim to some extremely large catfish. These known creatures have spooked several trained divers to the surface while working near the dam. If fact, the latent fear of nuclear contamination maybe to blame for the supposed sightings. Latent nuclear fears conjure up images reminiscent of some bad science fiction films of the 1950s like the *Creature from the Black Lagoon (1954)*. One never knows what might lay in the murky silt of a lake just waiting to burst forth from the calm placid waters.

Funky Factoid: The first *Pleasiosaurs* were believed to have appeared around 200 million years ago, and the last died out around 66 million years ago with the great Cretaceous-Paleogene Event.   **Note:** Lake Norman is North Carolina's largest manmade lake.

"Old School" Ghost Stories
(Case Study: Mooresville Senior High School)

In the early morning hours on August 1, 2008, a security camera caught a spectral image floating around in the old Asheville High School, in Asheville, North Carolina. The story made the news across much of Carolinas. Footage of this event can still be seen on the internet. I remember asking myself after seeing the news, "Was Asheville High School special in any way other than the fact that they had some tangible evidence of possible paranormal activity?"

Since the 19th Century there has been a fascination and attempted photographic documentation of the spirit world. Yet, since the advent of television series like the

Syfy Channel's: *Ghost Hunters* (first aired in 2004) and other like shows, there has been a resurgence of interest in the paranormal. There are many people who are divided on the methodology used by "ghost hunter" groups, and the results they present to a sometimes skeptical audience. With that being said, one still comes back to the original question. Was Asheville High School special for its reported paranormal activity?

The answer is a resounding No! Many schools, libraries, restaurants and hospitals regularly report strange activity. One of my students at Central Piedmont Community College told me she worked during the day at Hopewell High School. She stated that many people swear it is located on an old Native

American burial ground. Spooks have been reported by students and staff alike.

Take time to do general search online, and one will find literally thousands of hits across the internet. Entire websites and discussion boards are dedicated to "ghost hunting." I believe there is a simple fact: where there is a heavy flow of people in a central location long enough... strange stories are bound to occur at one time or another.

Schools are a particularly interesting place for paranormal activity to be reported. Many schools have certain "urban legends" which gets passed down over the generations that attend that specific institution. Mooreville, North Carolina has its own lore. Being that I have attended the Mooresville Graded School System as a student years ago, and now having taught there as a teacher for over 20 years, I have heard several classics. One persistent story is the "haunted gym" on the Magnolia Campus of Mooresville Senior High School.

Built during the late 1960s, this gym has hosted thousands of pep rallies, games, and gym classes. Since I was a student in the early 1980s stories of a phantom student have been reported lurking in the gym. It was said that this playful spirit liked basketball. I remember one story relayed to me by a former coach who was locking up after a late afternoon game. After stowing away the equipment, closing up the locker room, and turning out the lights he walked across the gym floor towards the exit. The coach said he clearly heard a voice saying "Do you want to play?" and the sound of a bouncing ball behind him. When he turned to look, no one was there. Needless to say, the coach probably broke the school sprinting record leaving the gym that night.

I had taught at the main campus in the old part of the high school for years, yet in 2014 I was relocated to the "Mag" as we all refer to it. Several months had passed as I settled into a new room directly down the hall from the gym. As October neared, and the season of Halloween approached, I realized that I could ask several people who would certainly know if there really was something to this local legend.

Many people do not realize how valued a good cup of coffee is to a teacher. The lounge is a sacred place in the mornings, and the coffee pot is a true friend on days that are full of testing, group projects, or just cold days coming in from the parking lot. It is also a chance to see people that you rarely get to see during a day of teaching, grading, running off papers, and inhaling lunch.

One day, just a few days before Halloween, I ran into one of our seasoned custodians getting his first cup of the day. It was early, and there were few people in the building. I casually asked him in my best skeptical and scientific demeanor, "Can I ask you a question, I have heard over the years that there was 'something' that goes bump in the gym… is there any truth to it?" Without hesitating, he said…

" I was in the office down stairs, and I was talking to one of the new guys about working here. No one other than us were in the building. I had just told him about the gym when we heard a ball bouncing right above us. The office is just below and off from the gym. He looked at me, and I looked at him stunned. I told him to run up the steps to see for himself that I was telling the truth."

After hearing this tale, I later talked to the new worker who said, " I ran up those stairs and there was not a soul in the gym when I opened the locked doors." He went on to say, "That wasn't the only thing that I have seen since I have been here. Lights cutting off and on and the like going on."

Whether or not the incidents of strange sounds, voices, or other occurrences in the Magnolia gym is a resident spirit, or a person's overly active imagination with a building that is reaching 50 years of age and settling, is purely up to each individual to decide. I have been in the school working by myself in the evenings before many times. Grading papers, or having to return to school to pick up something I forgot. To go back to school at night is the absolute worst. It is just plain scary when you are the only living soul in the building. As far as my take on the gym down the hall from my room, I have a healthy respect for the stories passed down to me. For the record: I am not going in there before or after hours!

Funky Factoid: Over 20 percent of Americans have claimed to have had a some form of paranormal experience with a ghost. The word "ghost" comes from the Germanic word *Geist* and/or *Gaistaz* meaning "spirit."

The Redcoats who Never Left

In 2014, I published a small book on a local battle during the American Revolutionary War which is entitled *A Quick and Bloody Affair: The Skirmish at Torrence's Tavern*. For many years it was thought that as Lord Cornwallis advanced across the Catawba River, the biggest battle between the British and local Patriot militia was at the water's edge at a place called Cowan's Ford. In this desperate fight, General William Lee Davidson lost his life while bravely trying to rally his men. After the British and German forces had crossed, they proceeded along a dusty road towards Salisbury, North Carolina. Several miles up this road, on the side of a intersection, lay a family owned inn called Torrence's Tavern.

For years, many of us 'locals' had heard this skirmish at the tavern was a small fight. A few men who had retreated from the ford were calming their nerves with a drink when the lead British cavalry elements showed up and surprised them. General Joseph Graham's account of this "skirmish" (which was one of only a few published accounts for many years) portrays this engagement as an almost afterthought to the Battle at Cowan's Ford. Yet, during my research I uncovered that this was a far larger and more brutal contest than was previously thought. Somewhere between 500 to 700 men were involved in this clash at the crossroads. Lt. Col. Banastre Tarleton commanded a tough legion of Tory Cavalry (Americans who supported the British) in the provincial forces that made up part of the British Southern Army.

It would have made a epic scene to have witnessed. Unlike General Graham's account of a few dazed militia being surprised, it was actually a large secondary line of defense with stationed forces waiting for the British to approach. Tarleton himself debated making a charge at this wall of determined men and overturned wagons beside the tavern. Yet, his reputation and ego forced him and his men to make a ferocious attack at the Patriot line which cost them both men and horses. It was yet another costly "sting" in the side of the British Army traveling through the hornet's nest of the Carolinas. The Patriots likewise suffered greatly. Many men were either trampled, or slashed in the head and back by sabres from the attacking Tory Legion.

It seems that battlefields have a certain mystique for the paranormal. I have heard many times that Gettysburg is the most haunted location in America. Possibly the energy and passions left in the wake of these terrible battles never quite leave. Men lost their lives fighting for something they believed in during these bloody engagements. Who is to say that this does not leave a trace behind?

I had just finished presenting my findings to the local Mary Slocumb Chapter of the DAR (Daughters of the American Revolution) when an elderly lady approached me from the audience. I was in the process of trying to get back to my little table in the back where I had fresh copies of my book for sale when I felt a light hand tug on my arm. I turned and noticed a petite lady who kindly complemented me on my research. She greatly enjoyed finding out the history of what she had heard about when she was a little girl growing up in the area off of Langtree Road where the battle had taken place. I told her it was my honor, and I was glad she enjoyed the presentation. However, as I was politely turning to go to my seat, she blindsided me with…

" I always wanted to know more about that battle. As a little girl, I heard at night the horses and men going up the road. Granny always said it was the ghosts of Cornwallis and his men."

By the time I had sat down and fully processed what I had heard, the lady had vanished into the bustling crowd. I was not able to get her name or number. Like the condemned spirits of the Tories that might still be haunting the road towards the tavern, the small elderly lady too had disappeared.

Funky Factoid: Not all British troops wore the famed "Red Coat." The cavalry under Col. Tarleton that attacked Torrence's Tavern wore the green "Royal Provincial" uniforms given to colonists that sided with the king. They were called "Tories."

The Ghost Who Caught his Killer: *North-Carolina Free Press* 1831 (A Syndicated Account)

Old newspapers are truly interesting to read. They are full of strange headlines, homemade medical remedies, church revivals, poems, national news and an occasional strange tale. While working on a graduate paper about Antebellum politics, I ran across a syndicated story in the July 12, 1831 of the *North-Carolina Free Press* that would certainly confound the legal system today. It was entitled: *Singular Circumstance,* it is a tale of an avenging spirit who prompts the living to catch his murderer. A modern *Hamlet* story if there ever was one.

The story tells of a distraught lady who went to a city alderman (city councilman) and fervently requested help. She told a strange and impassioned tale that she had been approached several times by the apparition of her husband who had died several years before. He had been a cattle driver or 'drover' who had been killed while away from home. The ghost had told her to seek out a specific policemen, and gave a detailed description of the person she was to get on the case of his death. Her pleas swayed the alderman to seek out the policeman (or constable) that she described. Much to his amazement, the alderman found the person she was describing. Both the lady and policeman swore that neither had ever laid eyes on the other, and something must be at work to bring them together on this unsolved case.

The lady described in detail what her dead husband had told her about the house where his murderer resided. The officer knew of just such a house, per her detailed description. It was located on an alley called Shippen Street. He was then able to obtain a search warrant (that would have been interesting to have heard from the judge's point of view). The house was soon raided by the authorities.

Upon arresting several men and a woman who were living in the house, one of the servants was reported to have said under his breath (referring to his master) "You will murder me as you did the drover," and the woman reported to have cried out: "Don't take me, I had no hand in the murder!" as they were dragged away to jail for further 'earthly' legal action.

Funky Factoid: Shakespeare's *Hamlet* is a story in which the ghost of the dead King of Denmark comes back to prompt his son (Hamlet) to seek revenge for his murder.

The Tricky "*Yehasuri*" of the Catawba Tribe.

Everybody has heard of the legendary leprechauns of Ireland. Due to countless stories pixies, fairies, and hobbits are now part of our collective culture. All of these tales tell of their magical powers and strange involvement with human kind. However, few that live outside of the Catawba Indian Nation have ever heard of the *Yehasuri*.

Like all parts of the world, the Native Americans have their own special lore and mythology. In many cultures, the belief in smaller human-like creatures exist. The Catawba Tribe have their own take on these mischief-minded supernatural beings. Much like the leprechauns of Ireland, the *Yehasuri* are said to be roughly two feet tall, and are rarely seen. They are said to live in the the woods and tall grasses, and eating what nature provides. If provoked, they can become aggressive, and fire small imperceptible arrows at their enemies.

I was fortunate to visit with an expert on the *Yehasuri* legend, Ms. Beckee Garris, on the Catawba Indian Nation Reservation in Rock Hill, South Carolina in early July of 2015. Beckee said the ancient people claim the *Yehasuri* had always existed since the beginning of the world. She stated at a young age children were taught to respect them, but they also learn several ways to avoid trouble with the mischief minded little people. Many Catawba would not allow grass to grow around their dwellings where the

Yehasuri could hide. Children's clothes, especially baby clothes, would not be left out on the line in the afternoon for it may make the *Yehasuir* curious, and possibly pester the child that night. One of the last tasks of the day for Catawba children is to sweep away their footprints outside of their homes, for the *Yehasuri* are sure to be drawn to them.

Like elves, the *Yehasuri* are always watching and keeping an eye on all of us "Big Folk." Beckee claimed that rocks or other small objects were sometime thrown by the *Yehasuri* at those that were not welcome on their lands. She also said that, "If the strangers were really bad, the *Yehasuri* would lead them off into the woods until they were really lost for good." A small prayer has been known to ward off the *Yehasuri,* yet Beckee said that only the Catawba know this charm which is still passed down from generation to generation. Though the *Yehasuri* were known for their mischief, they were also known to be guardians as well. Catawba children were told that as they grew up, the *Yehasuri* would look after them as they lived out their lives.

Today, the Catawba are still preserving their proud heritage. A new generation of Catawba youth are learning in the schools the Catawba language that has almost vanished due to five centuries of "cultural assimilation." In summer camps, children are fully immersed in the rich culture of Catawba art, pottery, and legends that have survived through the ages.

Funky Factoid: The Irish leprechaun has been reported since the Dark Ages. In some parts of Ireland he is said to wear a red (not green) outfit and hat. Some claim that this three foot creature is prone to hijinks for either good or evil purposes. The word *leprechaun* means "small body" in the Old Irish tongue.

The Devil's Tramping Ground: Fact or Fiction?

In the 1990s crop circles were a great fascination across the world. These mysterious flattened circles in the middle of grain fields started popping up in many countries. Though some of these circles are inexplicable to this day, many were proven to be manmade. Groups of people seeking public attention, started creating strange and intricate designs in remote areas in the evenings. Most of the groups were hoping to get a couple of moments featured on the local news broadcast.

Few people outside of North Carolina have noted that an isolated circle in the pine forests near the town of Bennet, has held the local public's fascination for decades. This strange circle is called "The Devils Tramping Ground." Since the early 20th Century, locals have claimed this barren patch has special powers. Some say objects in the circle can disappear, that vegetation does not grow, and that Satanic Rituals were held on the location years before and are the causes for such a strange phenomenon in the woods. Does the Devil go to this isolated place to plot the downfall of mankind in the epic battle between good and evil?

In July of 2015 I, along with my son, father, and a family friend and retired history teacher Steve Suther, made the trip to Chatham County to find the legendary spot. I will admit, since I was a young man I debated whether I really wanted to visit this piece of North Carolina folklore. Several friends had reported they camped at the circle on a dare. One of them coldly stated that in the dead of night, a strange ragged-looking man walked up into the camp. He politely asked if he could join them? Without waiting for an answer, he proceeded to walk right into the campfire; thus bursting into flames. Needless to say, my friends claimed they all left their gear, jumped into their car, and raced away fearing they had a true spectral encounter.

After getting a bit lost on the drive, a young local lady in a Jeep was kind enough to show us where the circle was located. It was not far from the main road, only about 50 yards. One could tell that many people had held parties and bonfires at the location. Beer cans and trash was strewn around the area. We measured the circle, and took soil samples going down several inches into the dirt and away from any bonfire ash. The entire circle was less than 60 feet in diameter and worn bare. As of now, the soil samples have been sent off to a lab for basic analysis. Other such samples taken by previous researchers have only yielded mixed results.

Nothing strange occurred during our investigation. Yet, it is a quiet place in the woods with only the sound of the pine trees rustling in the breeze. Rarely did a car go by. One could see how this desolate location could attract the attention of various groups over the years. If one looks at the newspapers of the 1920s when this anomaly was mentioned to the public, it is easy to find strange occurrences in the news. Remember, this was the era before news from across the world was readily available. We take it for granted today that if something happens in Asia, we will hear about it on CNN or the internet within a few minutes. Many times decades ago, editors were looking to add something to get the public's interest. More than one "tall tale" has been embellished to add a bit of spice to the local news.

No one knows why this specific spot was originally barren. One can only say that with continued use over the years as a camping location of why it stays mostly clear of vegetation. Interestingly, there were trails that led off behind the large circle. I decided to take a short walk down one of these trails just to see where it went. After about 60 yards in, and with no end in sight, I decided to return. To my surprise, my entire group was gone! A moment of fear gripped me like I had never felt before. Joyfully, I then heard the honk of a car horn just beyond the tree-line. They were ready to leave and get back to civilization and a good barbecue sandwich.

Funky Factoid: In 1678 it was reported in a British pamphlet about a "*Mowing-Devil: or Strange News outside of Hertford-Shire.*" It was said that the farmer did not want to pay the wages of the local men who usually cut the field of oats. He stated he would rather pay the devil than their high wage demands. That night a fire in the field could be seen, and in the morning it was found that the field was cut in a way that "no mortal could."

Staged photo of the "Witch of Shinnville"
(Shinnville, NC / Author's Archive)
Below: Grave of the Means family children
(Concord, NC / Author's Archive)

Lydia's Underpass... as Lyida would have appeared
(Jamestown, NC / Author's Archive)
Below: Lake Norman Charter School student Ryan Tuttle's
rendition of "Normie"

The Old "Mag" Gym at Mooresville Senior High
(Mooresville, NC /Author's Archive)
Below: Battle at Torrence's Tavern State Marker
(Mooresville, NC /Author's Archive)

The Devil's Tramping Grounds (Bennett, NC /Author's Archive)

Sources

Bertucci, Robert. "'Old School' Ghost Stories (Case Study: Mooresville Senior High School)" Interview by author. October 28, 2014.

"Child Spot Friendly Lake Norman Monster." *The Charlotte Observer.* Cabarrus. May 22, 2011. Accessed March 29, 2015. http://www.charlotteobserver.com/news/local/community/cabarrus/article9060113.html.

Garris, Beckee, (Interview) Catawba Indian Nation Reservation. 2 July, 2015. Rock Hill, South Carolina.

Largo, Jim, *Catawba Little People Picked on Children*, 10/27/2004 http://indiancountrytodaymedianetwork.com/2004/10/27/catawba-little-people-picked-children-94123 Retrieved: 03/02/2015

Lyons, Stephen. "The Legend of Loch Ness." NOVA. January 12, 1999. Accessed: March 27, 2015. http://www.pbs.org/wgbh/nova/ancient/legend-loch-ness.html.

"Old Crop Circles" http://oldcropcircles.weebly.com/uk-1678-hertfordshire.html (Retrieved: 01/03/2016).

"Singular Circumstance." *North-Carolina Free Press*, July 12, 1831.

Stonestreet, Chris. "A True Story Worthy of Mary Shelley's Frankenstein." *Mooresville Tribune*, October 28, 2009, Wednesday ed., Community sec.

_____ "Piedmont Ghost Legend: The Girl at the Underpass." *Mooresville Tribune*, October 23, 2011, Wednesday ed., Community sec.

_____ "The Witch of Shinnville: Legend Or..." *Mooresville Tribune*, October 30, 2013, Wednesday ed., Community sec.

Stonestreet III, O. C., "Summer of the Wampus," *The State* (July 1994).

Stonestreet IV, O.C., *A Quick and Bloody Affair: The Skirmish at Torrence's Tavern*, Createspace Publishing, Charleston SC, 2014.

"The Willowampus on the Warpath," *The Charlotte News*, August 15, 1911.

UNC-TV Science, *The Devil's Tramping Ground*, http://science.unctv.org/content/devil's-tramping-ground (Retrieved: 01/03/2016).

"Wampus Wandering thru South Iredell," *Mooresville Enterprise*, April 30, 1931.

Other Works by the Author:

The Battle of Cowan's Ford: General Davidson's Stand on the Catawba River, and its place in North Carolina History (2012)

The Battle of Colson's Mill: Death Knell of the Carolina Tories (2014)

A Quick and Bloody Affair: The Skirmish at Torrence's Tavern (2014)

www.ingramcontent.com/pod-product-compliance
Lightning Source LLC
Chambersburg PA
CBHW072110280526
45788CB00006B/2475